Ignacio's Chair

Gloria Evangelista
Illustrated by Cathy Morrison

Fulcrum Publishing
Golden, Colorado

This book is dedicated to my mom and dad,
who taught me to remember.
—G. E.

To my family—past, present, and future
—C. M.

Library of Congress Cataloging-in-Publication Data
Evangelista, Gloria.
   Ignacio's chair / Gloria Evangelista ; illustrated by Cathy Morrison.
      p. cm.
Summary: Through more than five centuries, an elaborate chair carved
by a Spanish monk is passed from one owner to another against the
backdrop of major world events, including the Spanish Armada, the
Civil War, and the Great Depression.
   ISBN 1-55591-966-9 (hardcover)
   1. Chairs—History—Juvenile literature. 2. World history—Juvenile
literature. 3. Material culture—Juvenile literature. [1. Chairs. 2.
World history.] I. Morrison, Cathy, ill. II. Title.
D210 .E95 2002
909—dc21
                                                                    2002003882

Printed in China
0 9 7 8 6 5 4 3 2 1

Design: Patty Maher
Editorial: Marlene Blessing, Daniel Forrest-Bank

Fulcrum Publishing
16100 Table Mountain Parkway, Suite 300
Golden, Colorado 80403
(800) 992-2908 • (303) 277-1623
www.fulcrum-books.com

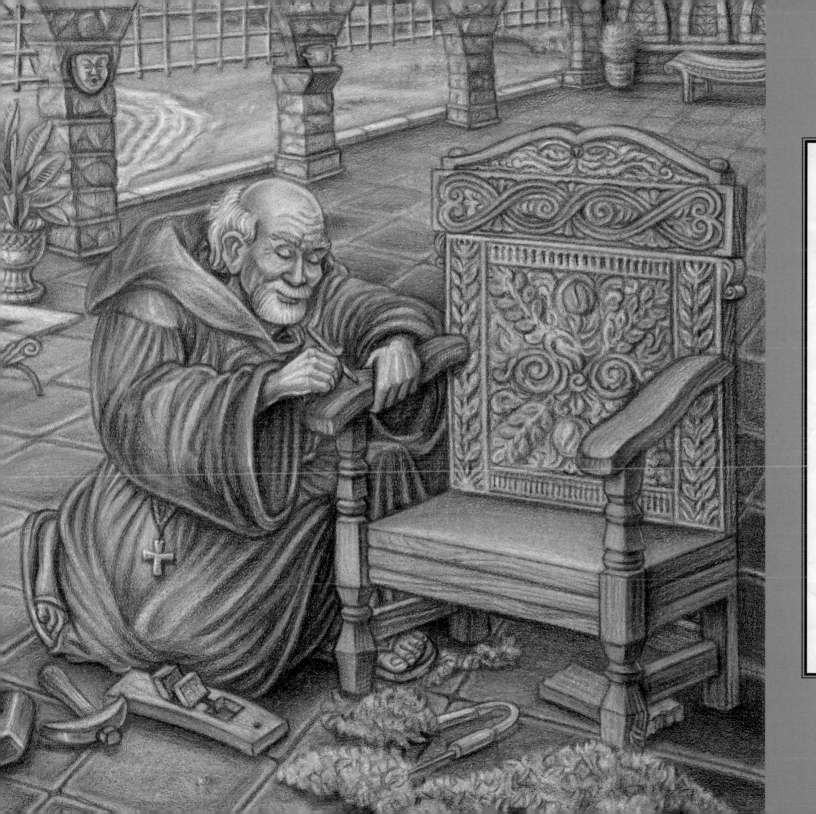

Long ago, across seas and centuries...

a frail monk struggled to carve a surprise for his bishop. He slept but a wink and ate little more, until finally, arising out of mounds of splinters and wood shavings, stood the most extraordinary chair.

Before his eyes
closed forever,
Ignacio whispered:

With all things past,
remember me.
I am a part of history.
Sit in my chair and
watch the sea.
With every wave,
wave back at me.

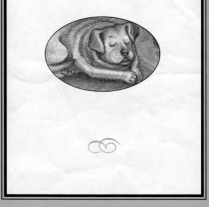

1492	1503	1509–1547	1519–1522
Italian-born navigator Christopher Columbus sails to New World	Italian Renaissance artist Leonardo da Vinci paints the *Mona Lisa*	Reign of England's King Henry VIII	Portuguese explorer Ferdinand Magellan completes first voyage around the world

The monastery was seized by the King of England. The chair so impressed him that he took it as his own. He sprawled in it as jesters joked, ladies waited, and dancers spun. He fingered its carved ivy pattern, which symbolized life without end, and believed that he alone would live forever.

∞

1531

Haley's Comet causes panic

English Reformation—monasteries robbed
and surrendered to king; treasures disappear

1537–1540

1543

Polish astronomer Nicolaus Copernicus
proves planets revolve around the sun

1558–1603

Reign of England's
Queen Elizabeth I

Ah, but a kingdom away, a greedy queen schemed to snatch the king's land. In darkness her soldiers rode their mighty horses, nostrils flaring, black eyes glaring, the hammering of hoofs echoing, blaring. They trampled the guards and charged the court, and the king flung the chair at the invaders and fled into the night.

1560

**Graphite discovered in England;
the first pencil made soon after**

1564

**English playwrite
William Shakespeare born**

First world map by Flemish
cartographer Mercator; coins the word "atlas"

1569

The chair dazzled the queen. She ruled from it daily as handmaidens powdered, servants buffed, and footmen fanned perfume into the air. Soon an explorer arrived, and on bended knee he petitioned his queen.

1577–1580

Sir Francis Drake sails for England; claims part of California for Queen Elizabeth I

1588

Defeat of the Spanish Armada by the British

Microscope invented by Dutch spectacle-maker Zacharias Jenssen

1590

1596

Equal sign (=) first used in mathematics

Surely a chair this grand would guarantee the respect of his crew. He promised the queen to find new lands, only asking in return for her blessing and the chair. The queen thought long and hard before she granted his wish.

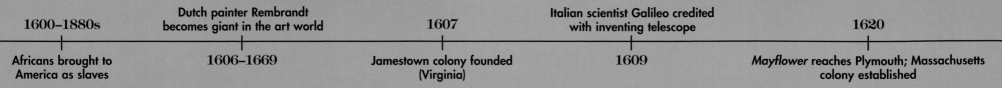

1600–1880s

Africans brought to America as slaves

Dutch painter Rembrandt becomes giant in the art world

1606–1669

1607

Jamestown colony founded (Virginia)

Italian scientist Galileo credited with inventing telescope

1609

1620

Mayflower reaches Plymouth; Massachusetts colony established

On deck, the explorer commanded from the chair as bodies hungered, mouths thirsted, and backs baked in the blistering sun.

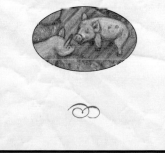

1621
First Thanksgiving between pilgrims and Native Americans

1625
New York colony established

Maryland colony established
1633

1636
Connecticut colony established

One night, pirates jumped his ship. They climbed the cables and swarmed the deck. They sneered and jeered and raised their hairy fists.

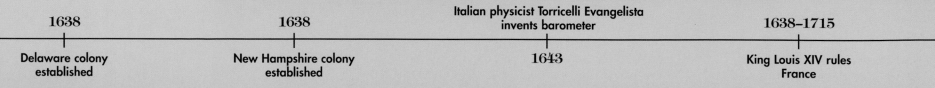

Italian physicist Torricelli Evangelista invents barometer

1638
Delaware colony established

1638
New Hampshire colony established

1643

1638–1715
King Louis XIV rules France

With greed reflected in glassy eyes, they piled the chair high with jewels, silver, and powder kegs, and hauled it away like some huge treasure chest.

∞

1650–1725

The Golden Age of Piracy—pirates seize
ships, acquire immense wealth

1653

North Carolina colony
established

Dutch astronomer Christiaan Huyens
invents pendulum clock; revolutionizes time-keeping

1656

The pirates landed on an island and traded the chair to a Native in exchange for barrels of salted fish.

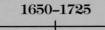

1650–1725	1663	New Jersey colony established	1666
Pirates use Caribbean Islands to stash treasures in coves, trade goods, and obtain fresh water and provisions	South Carolina established	1664	English astronomer Sir Issac Newton discovers Law of Gravity

ears later, an island fisherman found the chair abandoned in a jungle choked with breadfruit trees and coconut palms. He carted it to his home where he tossed rods against its back, hooks across its arms, and fish upon its seat. His parrot used the chair as a regal perch to belt out its lusty calls.

German philosopher and mathematician
Gottfried Leibniz invents mechanical calculator

1682

1690

1670

Pennsylvania colony
established

Massachusetts colony issues first
paper money in America

One day, the fisherman's son set sail for the New World. He had heard of great opportunities there. The fisherman painted the chair the color of the deep blue sea, gave it to his son, and said, *"Remember me."*

1700s

Natives of the Caribbean Islands who sought passage
to the New World often were forced into slavery once they arrived

1712

English tool seller Thomas Newcomen constructs
first steam-powered engine

As the ship neared shore, a storm exploded. The chair slid across the cabin floor and smashed into doors. Waves pounded, cargo spewed, barrels scattered, panic ensued. When the storm had cleared, the chair remained, battered but whole.

∽

1714
German physicist Daniel Fahrenheit invents mercury thermometer

1725
Beginning of Industrial Revolution

Georgia colony established

1732

1744–1792
King Louis XVI rules France

Upon landing, the fisherman's son was dragged to a slave market where families shivered, traders haggled, and freedom perished. The son refused to part with his chair, and so son and chair were bound and sold together.

1700–1800s

African laborers forced to work plantations
denied freedom because of race

American industrialist Benjamin Franklin flies
kite in thunderstorm to study lightning electricity

1750

1760

Belgium inventor Joseph Merlin
introduces first roller skate

"Boston Tea Party"—disguised colonists dump tea
into Boston Harbor in defiance of tax acts

1773

The chair was placed in the manor of a great plantation. There it remained as slaves toiled in fields of tobacco, shackles clinging, blisters bleeding, heads hung low softly singing songs of the Promised Land.

1775–1783
The Revolutionary War

July 4, 1776
Signing of the Declaration of Independence

German composer Ludwig von Beethoven writes first musical score

1782

1787
Signing of the U.S. Constitution

1789–1797
George Washington serves as first president of the United States

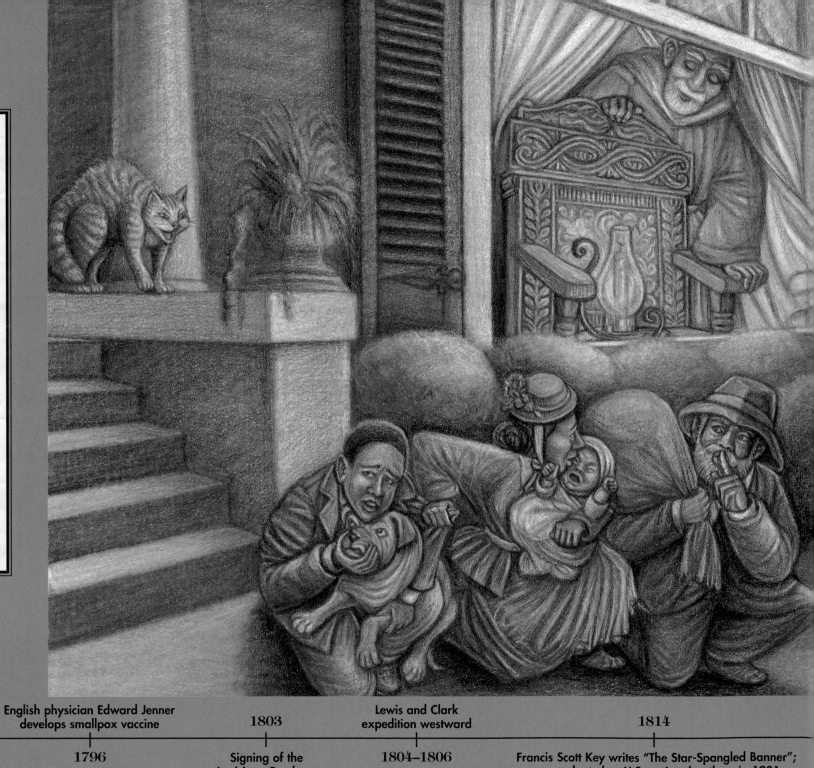

A scullery maid pushed the chair against a high window and set a lantern upon it, signaling that the hour had come. That night as the household slept, hushed slaves crept along an "Underground Railroad" to freedom.

1793

American inventor Eli Whitney invents cotton gin

English physician Edward Jenner develops smallpox vaccine

1796

1803

Signing of the Louisiana Purchase

Lewis and Clark expedition westward

1804–1806

1814

Francis Scott Key writes "The Star-Spangled Banner"; song adopted as U.S. national anthem in 1931

Not long after, war erupted at the manor's doorstep. The chair rattled as muskets crackled, cannons roared, and bullets rained on rooftops. The wounded wailed in dusty fields and soldiers collapsed in the chair.

1838

Trail of Tears: Cherokee people are forcibly moved west from North Carolina

Gold discovered at Sutter's Creek in California

1848

1849

Harriet Tubman escapes slavery on "Underground Railroad"

Abraham Lincoln becomes 16th president of the United States; 11 states secede Union, leading to Civil War.

1861

1861–1865

The U.S. Civil War—the South fights the North

Soon, blue-coated generals marched through Georgia and set Savannah afire. An officer spied the chair on top of a heap and yanked it away seconds before flames consumed it.

❧

1863

Battle of Gettysburg; Abraham Lincoln delivers "Gettysburg Address"

General Sherman's destructive "March to the Sea" ends Civil War; Abraham Lincoln assassinated

1865

1866

Union officers return North after Civil War and assume positions in government

Austrian monk Gregor Mendel discovers Law of Heredity

1866

After the war, the officer hauled the chair North with him. He positioned the chair at his desk and there New York's commissioner sat, year after year, directing his city's affairs.

1868

Scottish-born inventor Alexander Bell introduces telephone

1879

1886

New York City's subway system constructed in response to bulging population and traffic jams

1876

American inventor Thomas Edison introduces light bulb

Statue of Liberty given to the United States by France

When the commissioner retired, he bequeathed the chair to his nephew. The chair, now painted the color of night, stood dockside as the nephew's ship pulled into port. The silhouette of the towering lady captivated the new arrivals. To him and his young family, the statue signaled great things to come, and they whisked the chair away to the tiny tenement they would now call home.

1886
American pharmacist
John Pemberton invents Coca Cola

Ellis Island in New York; more
than 12 million people immigrate

1892–1954

1901

Italian physicist Guglielmo Marconi
transmits first wireless signal

Wright Brothers take flight in first human-powered
airplane, Kitty Hawk, North Carolina

1903

In the land of opportunity, the nephew found none. Soon his children grew hungry and his wife grew thin. He sold his knife for flour and his boots for milk. He sold his mattress for coal and his trunk for rent. When his wife became sick and needed medicine, he sold the chair.

1905
German-born physicist Albert Einstein discovers theory of relativity: E=mc²

American industrialist Henry Ford introduces the first mass-produced automobile, the Model T
1908

1914–1918
World War I

1929
New York stock market crashes, beginning the Great Depression

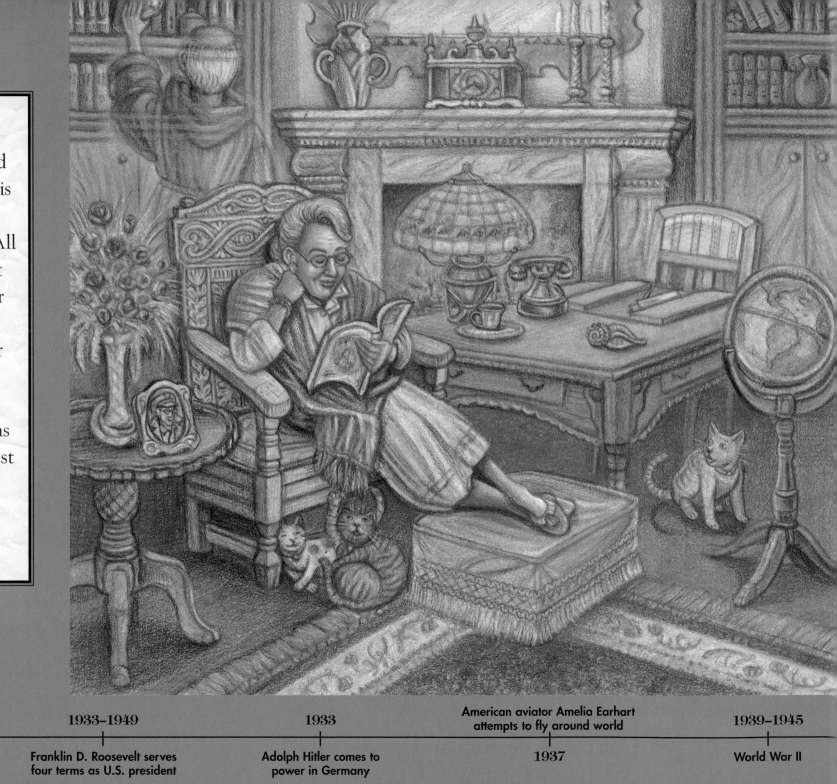

A widow offered to buy it. A chair this straight would be good for her back. All it needed was paint and a pillow. In her library, she relaxed by the fire with her books and her cats. The chair was as comforting to her as memories of the best days of her life.

1929
Mickey Mouse makes
screen debut

1933–1949
Franklin D. Roosevelt serves
four terms as U.S. president

1933
Adolph Hitler comes to
power in Germany

American aviator Amelia Earhart
attempts to fly around world
1937

1939–1945
World War II

The years passed. The woman moved in with her daughter, who stowed the old chair in the attic. There her grandchildren played on it and often spoke of an imaginary friend. Eventually the children grew up and their mother grew old.

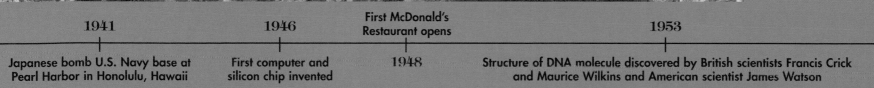

1941
Japanese bomb U.S. Navy base at
Pearl Harbor in Honolulu, Hawaii

1946
First computer and
silicon chip invented

First McDonald's
Restaurant opens

1948

1953
Structure of DNA molecule discovered by British scientists Francis Crick
and Maurice Wilkins and American scientist James Watson

1954–1975
Vietnam War

One day a man arrived at the mother's yard sale. He rummaged through platters, plates, and butter boats. He toyed with radios that did not speak and clocks with bronze horses that did not tick. When his eyes fell upon the chair, he knew he had found something of value.

1957

Soviets launch Sputnik-1;
space race begins

1961

John F. Kennedy becomes 35th
president of the United States

Neil Armstrong becomes first man
to walk on the moon

1969

1973

Indian occupation of
Wounded Knee, South Dakota

1979

Mount Saint Helens erupts
in Washington state

1981

Sally Ride becomes first
American woman in space

1986

Margaret Thatcher becomes first female
prime minister of Great Britain

1980

Personal computers (PC)
introduced by IBM

1983

Birthday of Martin Luther King, Jr.
becomes official U.S. holiday

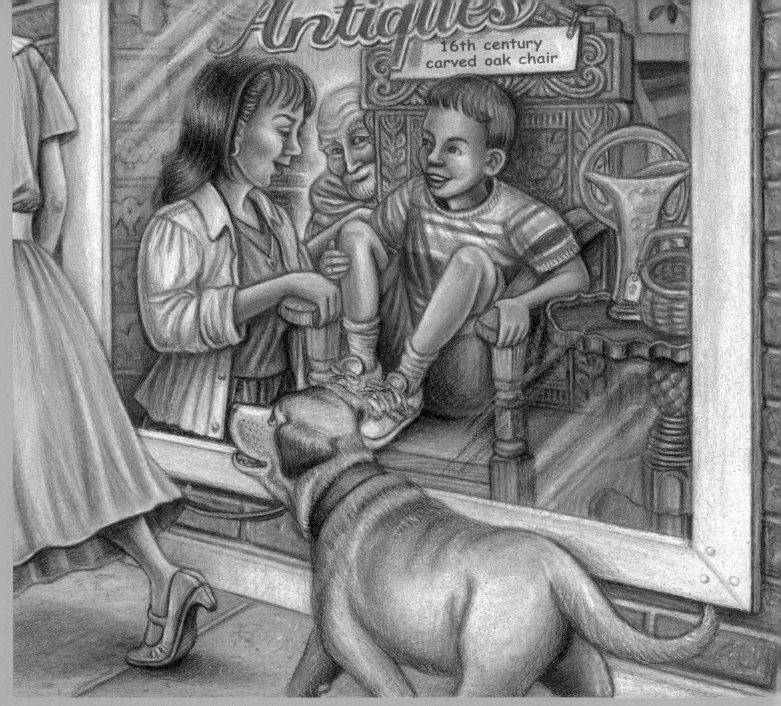

Soon a mother and son arrived and admired it. "This chair is rare," the mother said. "Perhaps one of a kind. I wonder what stories it would tell if it could." The boy's eyes flashed. His imagination soared. He fingered the chair's nicks and scratches. He sat in its well-worn seat, and within moments he was hugging the chair.

16th century carved oak chair

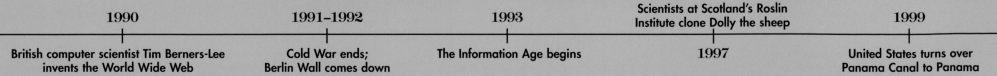

1990
British computer scientist Tim Berners-Lee invents the World Wide Web

1991–1992
Cold War ends; Berlin Wall comes down

1993
The Information Age begins

Scientists at Scotland's Roslin Institute clone Dolly the sheep
1997

1999
United States turns over Panama Canal to Panama

At home, the boy curled up in the chair, wondering about all the different people and places the chair might have touched over four hundred years. Of course, no one knew for sure. But that was okay, because to the boy the chair spoke a language all its own.

2000
New millennium; U.S. scientists publish first map of human gene sequence

2001
George W. Bush becomes 43rd president of the United States

2001
Hijacked jetliners topple twin towers at New York's World Trade Center and hit the U.S. Pentagon

With all things past, remember me. I am a part of history. Sit in my chair and watch the sea. With every wave, wave back at me.

And so it was.

The History of the Chair

In the Middle Ages, chairs were made only for royalty, nobility, the priesthood, and the wealthy classes. All others sat on stools or benches. The earliest English furniture of quality was made of oak imported from the Baltic Sea region, until the introduction of walnut from France in the middle of the seventeenth century. Furniture was made by hand until the Industrial Revolution in the late 1700s, when machinery was invented to save labor and increase production. Furniture, like the chair in the story, tells historians a great deal about everyday life in the past and indicates taste, artistic style, and the technological achievement of the age.

In the early 1600s, many Englishmen left their homes for opportunities in the New World. They were encouraged to bring tools, bedding, or glass for windows, because no markets existed to buy these items in the colonies. Most brought little with them. Nevertheless, a number of first-generation settlers left adequate estates, including chairs, chests, and tables, upon their deaths. Some of these furnishings were imported. Although not easy to come by, collectors can find pieces like the chair in the story that were made prior to the Elizabethan period, but they command high prices because they are rare.

Furniture made in America in the seventeenth century closely resembles furniture made in the parts of England and Europe, because that is where its craftsmen came from.

Today's furniture has many different styles. Advances in technology and new materials, such as plywood, fiberglass, and plastics, have played a part in its production. The machine-made chair now dominates, and only a few men and women continue to craft furniture by hand.

The Role of the Restorer

Most period pieces, like the chair in this story, have survived because the finish was maintained through waxing, repainting, and varnishing. These practices are shown in the book. In addition, old wood looks different than when new. It shrinks and swells, mostly in the direction across the grain, in response to changes in humidity and temperature, and often much of its original decoration has been lost. (Remember how the restorer in the story carves a new ear for the top of the chair's back seat and replaces its rotted feet?) It is also difficult to separate the original finish from finishes layered on over four centuries.